G000061575

Constellations

Glimpses of infinity in fact,
myth, and legend

By
Larry Sessions

Running Press
Philadelphia, Pennsylvania

Canadian representatives: General Publishing Co., Ltd.,
30 Lesmill Road, Don Mills, Ontario M3B 2T6.
International representatives: Worldwide Media
Services, Inc., 30 Montgomery Street, Jersey City, New
Jersey 07302.
Library of Congress Cataloging-in-Publication Number
92-50806
ISBN 1-56138-247-7
This book may be ordered by mail from the publisher.
Please include $1.00 for postage and handling.
But try your bookstore first!
Running Press Book Publishers
125 South Twenty-second Street
Philadelphia, Pennsylvania 19103

Contents

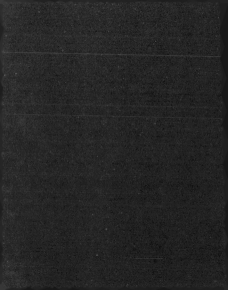

Introduction

Many cultures have contributed to the lore of the sky. Although the widely known classical mythology of the Greeks and Romans forms a varied backdrop for the study of the stars, other cultures have their own stories, beliefs, and myths. In fact, many stories about the constellations—especially those in the Southern Hemisphere—began to be told long after the classical world had become history.

Myths typically arose around the brightest and most easily-recognizable stars and constellations. The nine stars and constellations featured in this book were selected for the same reason. In addition, they were important enough for people to commemorate them with imaginative and enduring stories.

Three anomalies are included: one story, that of the constellation Boötes, is neither ancient nor a myth. Rather, it is a historical fact from the 20th century. The Pleiades, which is not recognized as a constellation in its own right but rather as a part of Taurus, is included because its fame far outshines that of the constellation of which it is a part. And the Milky Way is not a constellation at all, but is included because it is the stellar system to which all known constellations belong.

The final chapter of the book is designed to help you locate these constellations in the sky and to provide you with a few interesting facts about the stars—with the hope that you may be inspired to go out, observe, and imagine.

Orion,

The Hunter

Perhaps the most striking and magnificent constellation in all the heavens is this bright, well-defined, and easy-to-find winter constellation. Arranged in a large rectangle with three stars in a row in the middle, Orion is never forgotten once it is recognized.

Not surprisingly, there are many stories about this constellation, often identifying it with a human figure. Orion is best seen in the early evening sky of mid- to late-winter, standing upright in the south.

Orion typically was seen as a male figure, a warrior-god, hero, or great hunter. In ancient Egypt, Orion often was thought of as Osiris, the god of life, light, and the sun. In much of the Middle East he was the "Giant" or the "Strong One." The ancient Jews sometimes called these stars Nimrod, a biblical figure who was bound to the heavens for disobeying God. In India, Orion was a stag shot with an arrow (the three middle stars), while in China these stars were part of a constellation called the White Tiger. Some Brazilian Indians picture a cayman (a relative of alligators and crocodiles), and the Maoris of New Zealand saw a canoe.

Classical Mythology

Orion was a great and fearless hunter who fell in love with Merope, the daughter of a king named Oenopion. The king opposed the lovers' union and ordered Orion to be blinded and cast out to sea. At long last, the god Vulcan took pity on him and led him to the sky.

In another myth, Orion's arrogance angered the goddess Juno (though some say it was the Earth goddess, Gaia), who sent a scorpion to kill him. When he died, the moon goddess Diana (Artemis) placed him among the stars. The scorpion also was placed in the heavens, but on the opposite side of the sky so that it can never trouble Orion again.

Iroquois Myth

Long ago, there lived a man who had grown too old and feeble to hunt or do chores. He had become a burden to his family and an outcast to others. The old man knew that his days on Earth were dwindling, so with great effort he climbed a high mountain with his bundle on his back and his walking staff in his hand. When he reached the top, the old man began to sing his death chant, singing for a continuation of his spiritual journey—after life on earth.

His voice drifted down to his village below, where the people stopped what they were doing and turned their eyes to the lone figure on the moun-

taintop. As the people watched, the old man began to rise slowly into the air. As he rose, the old man's voice grew fainter and fainter. Soon, the people could not hear him at all. Finally, he took his place among the stars, where he can be seen even today as Old Man.

Old Man did not die, but assumed a new role. He gained back his strength and power, and now carries the sun across the sky in the summer. He knows how important the sun is, so he carries it high, bringing light and life to the crops and the people. But as the winter winds begin to blow, Old Man's muscles begin to ache under the strain, so he gives the burden to his son. Like many young people, Old Man's son tries to do the least work possible. He carries the sun low across the sky, making the days short and cold. At this time Old

Man can be seen at night, the bundle in which he had carried the sun dark and empty. But in spring he will take the sun back and carry it high again, bringing warmth and long days.

Tewa Myth

In the old times, the Tewa people relied on a great warrior and wise man called Long Sash. Once, when times were very bad, the people called out to Long Sash to deliver them. He led them across the Endless Path, the Milky Way.

Before long, the people grew tired and began to grumble. Long Sash stopped near the two bright stars the white man calls Gemini, the Twins, and demanded that the people follow him peacefully or go their own way. The people called the spot at which they had stopped the "Place of Decision." They decided to follow Long Sash.

But after a long, seemingly eternal journey, the people began to grumble and doubt Long Sash's ability again. They stopped, and Long Sash put down his headdress. The people called this spot the "Place of Doubt." After Long Sash had a good medicine dream in this place, he finally led his people to the "Middle Land," which is now their home forever. Long Sash lives there too, in the stars of Orion.

Even now his headdress can be seen
as the star group others call the Seven
Sisters, or the Pleiades.

Castor and Pollux, the two principal stars of this constellation, shine brightly and closely together in an otherwise dull part of the winter sky. They have been known almost universally as the Twins, the two figures, or by some other "couple" denotation.

To the Arabs they were the two peacocks; to the Chaldeans and Phoenicians they were the two kids (goats) or gazelles; and in Egypt they were sometimes called the two plants.

In China, the two stars represented various rivers and "swollen waters." (The ancient Chinese concern about the use of water is evident in many of their constellations.) Castor and Pollux were also said to represent the Chinese concepts of Yin and Yang—the contrasting dualities of life.

Classical Mythology

In classical mythology, Gemini—more specifically Castor and Pollux—were sons of the god Jupiter (Zeus) and the mortal Leda. They were brothers of the famed Helen of Troy, over whom the Trojan War was fought, and two of the Argonauts who sailed with Jason in search of the Golden Fleece. Castor and Pollux became the twin patrons of Rome and were especially revered by athletes, soldiers, and sailors.

Pollux was immortal, but his brother Castor was not. When Castor was killed in a fight over a fair maiden, his immortal brother grieved so much that he asked his father, Jupiter, to take him as well—but since Pollux was immortal, Jupiter could not let him die.

The King of the Gods compromised, however, and allowed the brothers to stay together. Half the time they would be in the underworld, the other half in the gods' abode. This is symbolized by the constellation's position in the sky: above the horizon half the time and below it the other half.

Blackfoot Myth

(In the following story, "Medicine" refers to spiritual or magical power. "Strong" or "big" medicine was favorable for the possessor; doing or making "bad" medicine was like courting catastrophe or disobeying one's personal spiritual guides.)

Once, a man named Smart Crow dreamt that a crow appeared and told him that his wife would bear him two sons. One son would grow up to be reliable and worthy, and the other disobedient. The crow also warned that one day, while his wife was alone, a stranger would appear at the lodge and try to kill her.

Not long after the dream, Smart Crow went off hunting. When he returned, he found his nightmare had

come true. His wife was dead and the two infants were alone in the lodge. Looking for revenge, he followed the trail of a stranger and soon found him. He was about to kill the stranger, when the stranger said, "I will restore your wife to you." Smart Crow did not believe him at first, but he wanted his wife back so badly that he let the stranger go and returned to the lodge.

There, he saw the two infants crying for food. He could not care for them alone, so he placed one on a rock and prayed to the rock to look after him. The other child he gave to his friend, the beaver, to raise.

So it was that the twin boys were raised by a rock and a beaver. When they were about six years old, Smart Crow wished to have them back. He found them in the woods and, after persuading them that he was their father, took them home with him. He named them Rock and Beaver. They performed a ceremony with the bones of the long-dead mother, who was then restored to life just as the stranger had promised.

Rock and Beaver then lived with their parents as normal children, except that they had strong medicine. Rock disobeyed his father and often talked Beaver into joining him. Once Rock shot an arrow at the Morning

Bird, who had big medicine. When Rock's arrow hit it, it fell on to the branch of a tree. Rock tried to reach it, but every time he got close, the bird got a little higher.

Beaver, who was still on the ground, could no longer see his brother, who had disappeared into the sky. Beaver was so afraid and ashamed that he decided he could not go home to face Smart Crow. Instead, he sat down under a tree and began to cry. Soon, an old woman heard the boy crying and took him to her lodge. There Beaver grew up, married, and became a leader of the people.

Beaver was a good and well-loved leader. But one day he was forced to leave his people. He had told his wife never to burn sagebrush in the fire, as this was bad medicine for him. Some time later she forgot and burned sage in the fire. Beaver could no longer live in this lodge. He took his white buffalo robe and went to look for his brother Rock. Beaver's medicine was strong now, and he soon found Rock high in the branches of the tree. From this high perch in the tree, they became stars, and now live forever in the sky. They are the twin stars that rise early in the winter.

Ursa Major,
The Great Bear

Though its stars are far from the brightest, the Great Bear, commonly known as the Big Dipper, is one of the most easily recognized constellations. In much of the Northern Hemisphere, Ursa Major is circumpolar, meaning it never sets and is visible every night of the year. The Blackfeet Indians and other tribes used this constellation as something of a clock, its stately turning around the North Celestial Pole marking the various times of night.

These stars have been known by many names around the world, including the Wagon (northwest Europe), the Plough (England), and Arthur's and Charles's Wains (referring to the chariots of England's King Arthur and France's Charlemagne, respectively). These names are logical, given the shape the stars form in the sky.

However, many cultures—Ancient Greeks, American Indian tribes, and the Eskimos, to name a few—knew

these stars as a bear, which requires a
more vivid imagination to visualize.
One common explanation is that the
constant circling around the North Celestial Pole suggests a prowling bear.
Here are three different tales.

Classical Mythology

Callisto was a beautiful maiden from Arcadia. Once, Jupiter (Zeus) noticed her in the forest and fell in love with her. When Jupiter's wife Juno (Hera) found out about her husband's infidelity, she turned Callisto into a bear, cursed to wander the forest forever.

Years later, Callisto's human son Arcas caught sight of the bear in the forest. Not knowing that it was his mother, Arcas aimed his deadly arrow

at her heart. But Jupiter quickly inter-
vened, flinging Callisto into the sky to
avoid the arrow. She stayed among
the stars to become Ursa Major, the
Great Bear. Jupiter flung Arcas into
the stars to become Ursa Minor, the
Smaller Bear.

In the sky, the Bears have long
tails. According to legend, Jupiter, in
flinging the two into the heavens,
grabbed them by the tails and swung
them over his head. In the process,

each tail stretched to the length we see today. Some American Indians also saw a bear in the stars of Ursa Major, and explained the unnatural length of its tail in a similar manner.

Greenland Eskimo Myth

Once, the child of an Eskimo woman died, and the woman grieved deeply. When she couldn't bear the pain any longer, she ran away from her village. Soon, she came upon a house with bear skins hanging in the passageway. She went in and found that the people of the house were really bears in human form. Despite this, she stayed with them for a time.

Eventually the woman became homesick and told the big bear that she would return to her own people.

"When you go to your home, tell no one about us," the bear told her, for the bear feared that men would come and kill her and her cubs.

When the woman returned to her home, she very much wanted to talk of what she had seen and where she had been. She resisted as best she could, but soon the urge to talk overcame her

and she told her husband of the bears. No sooner had she spoken than her husband called together the other men, and they went out to kill the bears.

The bear saw them coming, and managed to elude them long enough to find the woman's house and kill her. But the dogs caught the bear and closed in around it. Suddenly, the bear and the dogs started to glow and rose into the sky.

Thus came to be Qilugtussat, the

constellation that resembles dogs keep-
ing a bear at bay.

Aztec Myth

To the Aztecs, the god Quetzalcoatl was kind and helpful, teaching them many skills and virtues. But his brother Tezcatlipoca was a strife-monger and sorcerer who caused great trouble to humankind. Often he disguised himself as a jaguar, and in such disguise he once lost a leg when his enemies slammed a door on it. As a result, from then on he was forced to hop around on a wooden leg.

Once, Tezcatlipoca tried to destroy all of Quetzalcoatl's good deeds, which made Quetzalcoatl very angry. He turned his brother into a jaguar— then into a puppet. Finally, he placed him in the sky where he could no longer harm anyone.

Now a puppet, Tezcatlipoca must dance forever around the pole of the sky, on his peg leg when he is near the eastern horizon, on his hands when he is near the western horizon.

Boötes,
The Ploughman

To the modern eye, this constellation resembles a kite more than anything else, with the bright star Arcturus at the tail. In China, the stars of Boötes were seen as part of a huge dragon that stretched more than halfway across the sky. Arcturus was Ta Kio, the "Great Horn" of the dragon, arguably the most important star to the ancient Chinese.

In Egypt, this constellation was a benevolent goddess in the form of a hippopotamus. It was her duty to keep watch over the evil stars of the Thigh of Set, the constellation we call Ursa Major.

The Greeks and Romans had many names for these stars, including the Ox Driver, the Bear Watcher, and the Herdsman. The classical background tells the common story from Greece, and the American story is not a myth at all, but a true story about the star Arcturus.

Classical Mythology

The god of wine, Bacchus, once gave a grape grower named Icarius the secret of wine making. Icarius later invited many of his friends to a feast to sample the wine, and all the guests drank too much, awaking the next morning with terrible headaches. After talking, they decided that Icarius must have been trying to kill them all—so they killed him and threw his body in a ditch.

The grape grower's two dogs, missing their master, began to whine, and when Icarius's daughter let them free, they led her to her dead father's body. She was so distraught that she committed suicide.

All four were finally placed in the sky: Icarius became Boötes, his daughter Erigone became Virgo, and the two dogs became a faint constellation nearby, called Canes Venatici.

American Story

When planning began for the 1933 World's Fair, the Century of Progress Exposition to be held in Chicago, organizers began searching for a way to dramatize its opening. They realized that another World's Fair—the 1893 World's Columbian Exposition—was also held in Chicago. The promoters of the 1933 Fair, perhaps inspired by the concept of the Olympic Games, decided it would be a good idea to have a torch bearer to span the time from the previous Chicago World's Fair to their own. Unfortunately, no one had ignited a torch in 1893 for this purpose.

Resourcefully, the promoters turned to astronomy for help. At the time it was believed that the star Arcturus in Boötes was 40 light years from Earth. In other words, the light from Arcturus takes 40 years to reach Earth. The promoters reasoned that the light which originated on Arcturus in

1893, during the previous World's Fair, was just the torch flame they needed. This light would arrive at Earth just in time for the Century of Progress Exposition.

Astronomers used Galileo's original small telescope to focus the light from Arcturus onto a photocell, a then-new device that altered the flow of electricity when light shined on it. (It's the same kind of device still used for automatic door openers.)

On October 2, 1933, some of the light from Arcturus ended its long journey to Earth by falling through the lenses of Galileo's telescope and onto the photocell. The photocell acted as a switch to turn on the main spotlights that signaled the opening of the Exposition. In this way, the light from a distant star opened the show.

Scorpius

The Scorpion

Scorpius can be seen in the summer amid the glowing clouds of the Milky Way. Because it is so far south, the complete constellation can be seen above the horizon for only a short time in the Northern Hemisphere. It is at its best around 10 P.M. (Daylight Saving Time) in mid-July.

Many Indonesians see a palm tree in these stars, while this constellation sometimes was seen as a snake in Java and Brazil. To the Maya it may have

been the "sign of the death god." In
early China these stars were part of the
"Azure Dragon" and later the residence
of the "Blue Emperor," but in the early
Chinese zodiac it was the Hare.

Classical Mythology

Long ago, Juno sent a scorpion to sting the hunter Orion, who had arrogantly boasted that he would kill all the wild animals of Earth. The sting wounded Orion mortally, and Juno placed the Scorpion in the sky to warn others against such arrogance. Later, Orion was also placed in the sky but he always sets in the west as the Scorpion rises.

Hawaiian Myth

The trickster god, Maui, was not much
of a fisherman. His brothers often ridi-
culed him for failing to catch big fish.
But Maui found revenge by tricking his
brothers into giving up the fish that they
had hooked.

Maui's ancestors had given him a
magic hook made out of a jaw bone. It
was called Manaia-ka-lani (*Come here
from the heavens*). Maui knew the hook
would be used for some great purpose,

so he hid it away instead of using it for everyday fishing.

One day, Maui's brothers came back from a day's fishing with a poor catch. Maui boasted that they would have done better had he been with them. The next day, they took him out to the good fishing waters in their canoe. "Where are the big fish, Maui?" they chided.

By now, Maui was tired of their

teasing and decided to do something about it. He fitted the line with his magic hook, and baited it with an alae bird sacred to his mother, the goddess Hina. Maui threw the line as far as he could, far out over the horizon.

The magic hook hit the water and sank deep. Before long, Maui knew he had caught something big. The sea floor began to heave and great waves broke over the canoe. Maui called his brothers to help him pull in the huge fish, even as they fought to keep their canoe from capsizing.

For two days they fought to keep the line taut. Finally, the giant fish rose out of the waters and frightened them all. Maui warned his brothers not to look back or they would lose fish and canoe.

But this was no ordinary fish. It was larger than any island. For just one moment, one of the brothers looked back—he was so afraid that he let the line go slack and it broke. The giant fish flew off and crashed into the land, forming the island chain called Hawaii. The fish hook was flung far into the sky, where it became stuck and can now be seen outlined in stars.

The island nearest to where the brothers were fishing was named after Maui. Even today people recognize this fishing spot—just off the eastern coast of the island—straight out to sea at a place called Kaiwio Pele, south of the town of Hana.

Tahitian Myth

Once, there was a boy named Pipiri who had a sister named Rehua. Their parents called them Pipiri-ma. One night after they had gone to bed, their parents went fishing by torch-light. After a good catch, they returned and began roasting some fish for a late supper.

The alluring smell of the fish woke the children, but being well-behaved, they waited in bed until they were called. Their mother wanted to call the children, but their father felt it was best that they get their sleep. He told his wife not to awaken them.

The children overheard their parents' conversation and were very disappointed that they would not share in the meal. With their bellies growling and their feelings hurt, the children decided to run away. They slipped away without a sound. When Pipiri and Rehua's parents finished their meal, their mother went to check on them. She found they were missing, called to their father, and began to search.

"Oh Pipiri-ma!" the sad parents cried, "Pipiri-ma, return to us."

The children heard the calls, but did not return because they were angry and hurt. Instead, they caught a ride on a flying stag beetle which carried

them up to the skies. They became the last two stars at the barb of Maui's Fish Hook, the star group also known as the Scorpion. The stag beetle became the flaming red star known as Antares.

Lyra, The Harp
and
Aquila, The Eagle

Lyra is a compact constellation and
with its sparkling blue-white star, Vega,
it's one of the easiest to find in the
summer sky. It stands just at the western edge of the summer Milky Way.
Throughout most of the classical world
it was known as a lyre, harp, or another
stringed instrument. Other myths con-
jure up the vision of a bird (an eagle or
vulture in India, or a goose to some
Arab sky watchers).

Aquila, across the Milky Way from

Lyra, was commonly seen as an eagle or some other bird of prey. But in China, it was thought of as oxen, and to the inhabitants of India the three brightest stars of Aquila were the footprints of the god Vishnu.

The Japanese myth of these two constellations originated in China and appears with minor variations in Korea. In this myth, Tanabata is the name given to the star Vega, while Altair, the bright star of Aquila, is the peasant boy who became Tanabata's husband. In this tale the River of Heaven is the Milky Way.

Classical Mythology

Classical mythology tells that the lyre was invented by Mercury (Hermes)— he attached strings to an empty tortoise shell. Later, he traded it to Apollo, who gave it to his son Orpheus. Orpheus eventually became a great musician.

Aquila was the royal eagle of Jupiter, whose talons carried the mighty thunderbolts the King of the Gods hurled at the Titans.

Japanese Myth

There was once a beautiful Princess of Heaven named Tanabata, who loved to sit all day at her loom, weaving the glistening celestial fabric which adorned her most august and honorable father, the Emperor of Heaven. For many, many years there was nothing that gave her more pleasure than weaving the heavenly fabric.

One day, a peasant boy passed by, leading an ox. Tanabata looked up, their eyes met, and the warm rush of sudden affection filled both their hearts.

From then on, Tanabata cared no more for her weaving. All her thoughts were with the peasant boy who led his ox from star to star. Everyone in the kingdom of heaven could see that Tanabata had lost her love of weaving, and soon her most venerable father realized why. He went to her one day and told her that he would send for the ox boy, whose name was Hikoboshi,

that they might wed. Tanabata smiled
once again and bowed deeply to her
most revered parent.

Tanabata and Hikoboshi were
married with great joy and celebration.
They grew so close that they could not
stand to be apart for even one hour.
Hikoboshi began to neglect his ox, and
the animal wandered across the heavens, grazing here and there as it pleased.
Tanabata still neglected her duties, now
preferring to hold hands and gaze into

Hikoboshi's eyes rather than weave celestial cloth.

Soon, their neglect became intolerable to Tanabata's illustrious father, and he passed a harsh sentence on the two. Tanabata and Hikoboshi, he said, would be separated on opposite shores of the great River of Heaven. But the most praiseworthy Emperor was compassionate. He decreed that Hikoboshi would be allowed to cross the River of Heaven one night a year, on the seventh day of the seventh month.

And so, each year in Japan, the Festival of Tanabata celebrates the annual reunion of the two lovers in the sky. But if it rains on that night, the people of Japan call it the rain of tears, for the River of Heaven will be too rough for Hikoboshi to cross. The two must then wait patiently another year.

The Pleiades,
The Seven Sisters

Officially, the Pleiades do not form a separate constellation, but are a part of Taurus, the Bull. Through the ages, this tiny patch of stars has been far more important than the constellation in which they reside. The idea that these stars represent seven brothers, or more commonly seven sisters, is understandable, although you will need sharper-than-average eyesight today to see more than six of them. Perhaps one of the stars has faded, contributing to the myth of the Lost Pleiade.

Both classical writers and story-tellers among the Nez Perce Indians tell of the seventh sister, who fell in love with a mortal, was shamed by her love, and finally hid herself from view. Of course, it could be argued that the Nez Perce version might have resulted from the influence of early European contact.

Often associated with death, this tiny group of stars was particularly important in pre-Columbian Central America. The Aztecs feared that the world would come to an end when the Pleiades reached their highest point in the sky at midnight and the sacred and secular calendars coincided. This occurred every 52 years. There was a great deal of trepidation in the Aztec world when these circumstances occurred concurrently. However, human sacrifice always seemed to avert the danger for another 52 years, at least until the coming of the Europeans.

Classical Mythology

The seven Pleiades were the daughters of Atlas and Pleione. When Atlas was condemned to carry the weight of the Earth on his back, his daughters grieved so much that Jupiter took pity on them and changed them into stars.

Others claim that Orion once saw the seven sisters in the woods and fell in love with them. He began to chase them, and they cried out for help. Jupiter took pity on them, changed them

into a flock of doves, and placed them
in the sky.

Kiowa Myth

Once, seven little girls were playing and wandered off from their village. They played happily and did not see that they were getting far away from their tipis. Soon, a group of bears came along and, seeing the little girls, began to chase them. The seven little ones were too far away to run back to their village and too slow to outrun the bears. All they could do was to climb on top of a small boulder and pray to the rock to save them.

These little ones were good at heart, and the spirit of the rock heard their prayer. Suddenly the rock began to grow, carrying the seven girls into the sky. The bears rushed up to the rock and began to climb. But by then, it was too steep. Their claws dug into the rock, leaving deep grooves as the rock grew. But it was no use—they could not get the sisters.

The rock grew very high, and when it stopped, the seven little girls were transformed into stars and took their places in the sky, where we can see them still. The rock that grew can also still be seen. The Kiowa call it Mateo Tipi, but in English it is known as Devil's Tower, located in Wyoming.

Mayan Myth

Long ago, the heavenly twins Hun-Apu and Xbalanque were feuding with the mischievous giant Zipacna. One day, the twins enlisted the help of several other youths to dig a deep hole which, they told Zipacna, was to be the foundation of a very strong and secure house. But they couldn't seem to dig it deep enough.

They talked Zipacna into going into the pit to dig it deeper. As the giant reached the bottom, Hun-Apu, Xbalanque, and the others surprised him by hurling rocks, dirt, and even tree trunks into the pit. The giant was stunned, and he lay quiet as the pit filled over him. The brothers and their helpers, thinking that Zipacna was dead, finished the house. But he was not dead—he was waiting.

Zipacna waited until the house was complete and the brothers and friends had gathered there for a celebration.

Suddenly the giant rose up from the pit with such fury that the house, the twins, and all their helpers were flung up into the sky, where they got stuck against the vault of the heavens. They reside there today in a small cluster of stars.

Australian Aboriginal Myth

One day, while out walking, a man named Wurrunna came across the camp of seven young women. He stayed with them a while and, being lonely, decided that he was ready for a wife. He planned to catch two of the young women and take them with him. Wurrunna waited until the women took their digging sticks and went out to dig yams. As the women ate the yams they had found, Wurrunna quietly stole away with two of their digging sticks.

When they had finished eating, the five who still had their sticks went on, but the two without their sticks stayed behind, thinking that they had misplaced them. Wurrunna burst out of his hiding place and grabbed the two young women.

Weeks passed, and the two women

finally seemed to have accepted their fate as Wurrunna's wives. One day, he ordered them to gather bark for the fire from certain trees near their camp. The wives told Wurrunna that if they took the bark, he would never see them again. He told them that they could never escape and to go get the bark. The two wives took their stone axes and began to cut bark from the trees.

As soon as each woman had planted her axe into a tree, the trees began to rise, carrying the two women with them. Wurrunna could not reach them, and his two wives would not come down. Before long, the trees had reached the sky and the two girls met their five friends, who were already there. They all came together to live forever in the sky as the group of stars the Daen blackfellows call Maya-mayi.

Via Lactea,

The Milky Way

The Milky Way deserves recognition in any book about the mythology of the night sky, even though it isn't a constellation. Not surprisingly, many people around the world have seen our galaxy as a river of stars.

In India it was viewed as a celestial equivalent of the sacred Ganges, or sometimes as the Path of the Snake. The Thais named it the Road of the White Elephant, and in Mongolia it was perceived as the seam where the two halves of the sky were sewn together. The Sumerians thought it was a Great Serpent, and people from the Eskimos to the Bushmen of Africa called it a Track of Ashes.

The Iroquois Indians thought of the Milky Way as the Pathway to Heaven, while the Kiowa, Cheyenne, and other plains tribes imagined it as the track where the horse and the buffalo once raced across the skies. The Finns and Lithuanians named the

galaxy the Birds' Way, and in Poly-
nesia it sometimes was seen as a great
cloud-eating shark.

Classical Mythology

Hercules was the illegitimate son of
Jupiter and Alcmena, a mortal. The
King of the Gods hoped to give his son
immortality by letting him suckle at

the breast of his wife, the goddess Juno. So he laid Hercules next to Juno as she slept. Hercules, as an infant already exhibiting his legendary strength, suckled so vigorously that he woke Juno up and she, not pleased at the reminder of Jupiter's infidelity, pulled away with a jerk. Some of the milk spurted out and spread across the sky forming the Milky Way. This starry path was also thought of as the main street of heaven.

Estonian Myth

There once lived a beautiful young woman named Lindu, daughter of Uko, the god of the sky and thunder. Lindu cared for the birds, making sure that their seasonal passages were safe and appointing them places to dwell. She was well loved by all.

All the young men wanted to marry Lindu, but she was very particular. Once, the North Star came to her in all his finery and proposed to her.

"You always stay in one place and cannot even move away from it," she told him. "That is too dull for me. I cannot marry you."

She rejected the Sun, who was too constant, and the Moon, who was too changeable. It looked as if no one could please her. Finally, the Northern Lights came to call—in a diamond coach drawn by a thousand white horses. His gifts were dazzling, and more numerous and desirable than those she had received before. The Northern Lights pleased Lindu. She liked the way he danced across the sky, and how he always looked beautiful.

"You are not always the same," she told him. "You come and go as you please, and you are always arrayed in a beautiful new robe whenever you appear. You are the suitor I will marry."

So Lindu and the Northern Lights celebrated their betrothal as the Sun, Moon, and North Star looked on wistfully. But the Northern Lights could not stay long, saying that he was obliged to return north around midnight. As he left, he promised to return soon for the wedding.

The following day came and went without the return of the Northern Lights. Another day passed, and another—until it was obvious that he would not return. Lindu sat in the meadow in her wedding gown and grew ever more sorrowful, constantly forgetful of her duties to the birds. Finally, her father, Uko, could bear it no longer. He called the winds—to lift her gently to the sky. She is still there today, her bridal veil flowing from one side of the sky to the other.

Shoshone Myth

Back in the days of creation, there lived a grizzly bear named Wakim. He was a great bear, strong and wise in the ways of nature, but he once lost a fight and was banished to the Land of Souls. To get to this land, Wakim had to climb a great mountain. But Wakim did not want to go there, for he feared that he would miss the hunt, the sweet berries, and all the other things he loved so much on Earth. But he had to obey the laws of the wild, and he began to climb the mountain.

It was not an easy climb, and Wakim did not hurry. Soon, it began to snow. At first, the snowflakes fell lightly, but the snow gradually appeared in great quantities, covering the ground, the trees, and the rocks. A white layer of snow began to collect on Wakim's thick, shaggy coat.

Finally, Wakim passed the point where trees no longer grew. Off in the distance, just beyond the top of the mountain, he could see the Land of Souls. When he saw it with his own eyes, the Land of Souls did not look like the miserable place he had imagined. In fact, Wakim picked up his pace and was soon running. When he reached the top of the mountain, Wakim was running so fast that he flew off—right up to the Land of Souls! As he flew, the snow that had collected on his coat fell off, leaving a sparkling trail across the sky. We can still see this trail today.

Star Guide

As the Earth turns on its axis, all celestial objects appear to rise in the east and set in the west. Roughly six hours after a star rises, it crosses an imaginary line drawn from a point due north to a point due south. This imaginary line is called the observer's meridian. The original definition of noon was the time at which the sun crosses the observer's meridian. At that point in the day, the sun reaches its highest point in the sky. For this reason, it was called "high noon." Modern practice has made this definition obsolete, but it is helpful in constellation viewing if you think of a star as having its "noon" when it crosses, or transits, the meridian.

Each night, stars rise four minutes earlier than the night before. This happens because in addition to turning on its axis every day, the Earth also travels around the sun. During its yearly revolution, the Earth's orientation to the stars—and sun—changes. In the course of one month, the four-minute per day difference accumulates to about 120 minutes, or two hours. It doesn't take much figuring to realize that if a star rises at 6:00 P.M. on the first of January, six months later it will be rising at 6:00 A.M. So, on July 1, instead of rising at 6:00 P.M. that star sets at that

to the four cardinal point directions.

To more easily find your way around the night sky, read the following section in its entirety; there are many nuggets of information you might otherwise miss. Then go back and read the portions relating to the constellations that most strike your interest.

Orion

Orion transits about 10:00 P.M. in mid-January. At this time of year, the Belt of Orion stands about 50° high above the southern horizon (for observers around 40° north latitude). The bright orangish-red star which marks Orion's right shoulder is Betelgeuse (usually pronounced "beetle juice," though more correctly "bet'-el-juuz").

There is some disagreement as to Orion's distance from Earth, with estimates ranging from 300 to 650 light years away. (A light year is the distance a beam of light travels in one year at the speed of 186,282.397 miles per second. That comes to nearly six trillion miles in a year.) Even if Betelgeuse is only 300 light years away, to be seen it must be more than 500 million miles in diameter (nearly six hundred times the diameter of the sun).

In the opposite corner of Orion's rectangle is bright blue Rigel ("Rye'jell"). It is thought to be about 900 light years away and 50 times the diameter of the sun. The blue-white

color indicates that it is about 22,000°
F, much hotter than our sun (10,000°
F) or red Betelgeuse (5,500° F). In
general, the color of a star indicates its
surface temperature. Blue stars are hot-
test and red stars coolest; other colors
of the spectrum indicate intermediate
temperatures.

Approximately between Betelgeuse and Rigel are three stars in a
row, known as the Belt of Orion. Be-

neath those three stars are several fainter stars in the Sword of Orion. Near the tip of the sword is a faint smudge of light known as M42, or the Great Orion Nebula. M42 is an immense cloud of gases and dust from which new stars are being born. About 1,600 light years away and about 15 light years across, this beautiful nebula can be seen through binoculars or small telescopes.

About 100 objects within the constellations are referred to as "M" objects, such as M31, M42, or M45. These objects are designated in honor of the French comet hunter Charles Messier. "M" objects are star clusters, galaxies, and clouds of interstellar gas and dust (nebulae). In a small telescope, "M" objects appear similar to comets. Messier compiled the initial version of the list so he wouldn't confuse them with comets in the future.

Gemini

Look for these stars high overhead (about 80° altitude) at 10:00 P.M. in mid-February. Castor, 45 light years away, is slightly dimmer than Pollux. A small telescope will reveal that Castor is a double star, while more sensitive instruments reveal six stars where we discern only one with the naked eye.

Pollux is a giant orange star, slightly brighter than Castor and approximately 35 light years from Earth.

Ursa Major

Throughout most of North America, Ursa Major is visible all night. The stars transit at 10:00 P.M. (Daylight Saving Time) around the end of April and beginning of May. The two stars at the end of the bowl of the Dipper point to Polaris, the North Star. If you draw a curving line in the sky, directly along the handle but away from the Dipper, you will come to Arcturus in Boötes. Think of the curve of the Dipper's handle as an arc. Then "arc to Arcturus."

Near the middle of the Dipper's handle is a double star—Mizar and Alcor. Under reasonably good conditions, these stars are visible to the unaided eye. The ability to discern Alcor from Mizar's glare was once considered an accomplishment of excellent vision. Perhaps the star has grown brighter or moved farther from Mizar, for under good conditions the sighting of Alcor is fairly commonplace

today. There are also several galaxies
in Ursa Major, denoted by "M" numbers, which may be faintly visible
through binoculars.

Boötes

Boötes transits at 10:00 P.M. (Daylight
Saving Time) in mid-June, at an altitude of 70° to 80°. Arcturus is between
34 and 36 light years away. An orange
star with a diameter roughly 25 times

that of the sun, it is the brightest star in the northern half of the sky and the fourth brightest star in the heavens.

Scientists have measured the amount of heat received from Arcturus and found it only to be equal to the heat of a single candle at a distance of five miles!

Scorpius

Scorpius transits around 10:00 P.M. (Daylight Saving Time) in mid-July. Antares, the brightest star in the constellation, rises less than 25° in altitude for observers at 40° north latitude. The name Antares comes from the Greek word, meaning "Rivaling Mars." This is because the star's orange color is reminiscent of the planet's hue. A supergiant star—with a diameter nearly 600 times that of our sun—Antares is about 520 light years away. If you placed it where the sun is in our solar system, Antares would engulf Mercury, Venus, Earth, and Mars, and its surface would extend more than halfway out to the orbit of Jupiter.

This constellation is also full of double stars and star clusters, some of which are visible to the unaided eye. The clusters are designated with "M" and "NGC" numbers.

Lyra and Aquila

Lyra transits at 10:00 P.M. (Daylight Saving Time) in mid- to late-August. Aquila does the same in early September. Lyra rises almost directly overhead to nearly 90°. Aquila's bright star, Altair, rises to nearly 60° above the southern horizon. Vega in Lyra, about 26 light years away, is the fifth brightest star in the sky. Altair isn't as bright, but it is just 16 light years from Earth. Along

with another bright star to the north-
east, Deneb in Cygnus, these stars form
a prominent grouping known as the
Summer Triangle.

Epsilon, a star in Lyra, possesses a
"double nature" that may be discerned
by the human eye under excellent conditions. Telescopes reveal that each of
the two stars is double, making it a
"double double."

The Pleiades

The Pleiades transit at 10:00 P.M. just before Christmas. The constellation will be nearly 75° high in the heavens. The cluster contains several hundred stars, many of which are visible through binoculars or a small telescope. All of the stars are bound to the cluster by gravity. The Pleiades were number 45 on Messier's list, although it is hard to imagine how anyone could mistake this cluster for a comet. There is much interstellar dust around these stars, however, which reflects the starlight and makes the whole cluster slightly fuzzy in appearance. The Pleiades are about 415 light years away.

A bit farther to the east, near the star Aldebaran in the face of Taurus the Bull, is another star cluster called the Hyades. These stars are more spread out and much less striking than the Pleiades.

Via Lactea

Entire books have been written about the Milky Way galaxy. Approximately 100,000 light years across, it looks like a huge disk composed of over 100 billion stars. Our sun is located two-thirds to three-quarters of the way out from the center of the galaxy. Except for those that are relatively close to us, the stars of the Milky Way are so distant that their light simply blends together, causing a milky glow. We see it as a band of light because we are inside it. When we look down at the flat part of the disk, we see a much higher concentration of stars. And when we look away from the Milky Way, the stars we see are also part of it—we're just not looking in the direction in which they are concentrated.

The Milky Way is best seen in the summer, shortly after dark when it crosses the sky from north to south. At this time you may also see a "Great Rift" of dark material, causing the Milky Way to appear to be split into two sections. This is caused by dark clouds of matter in the Milky Way.

☪

The stories in this book have been collected over the past 20 years from a wide variety of sources. I can take credit only for the order and interpretation with which they are presented here. The true credit goes to those intrepid astronomers, anthropologists, and scribes who first sought to collect and preserve the thoughts and beliefs of cultures which are now largely extinct.

This book has been bound
using handcraft methods, and
Smyth-sewn to ensure durability.
The dust jacket and interior were designed by
Stephanie Longo.
The dust jacket and interior wood engravings
are by Clare Hemstock.
The wheel line art is by Helen I. Driggs.
The text was edited by David Borgenicht
and Cynthia L. Gitter.
The text was set in Minister Light by
Richard Conklin.
The book is printed in Hong Kong by
South Sea Int'l Press Ltd.